Dedicated to

With love from

Presented on

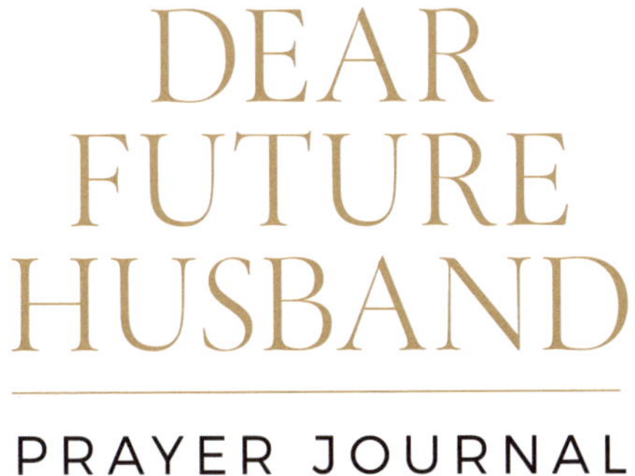

PRAYER JOURNAL

Trusting God with Your Love Story

Dear Future Husband Prayer Journal

Published by Thomas Nelson, 501 Nelson Place, Nashville, TN 37214, USA. Thomas Nelson is a registered trademark of HarperCollins Christian Publishing, Inc.

Thomas Nelson titles may be purchased in bulk for educational, business, fundraising or sales promotional use. For information, please email SpecialMarkets@ThomasNelson.com.

ISBN 978-1-4002-5633-4 (HC)

HarperCollins Publishers, Macken House, 39/40 Mayor Street Upper, Dublin 1, D01 C9W8, Ireland (https://www.harpercollins.com)

Cover design: Greg Jackson, Think Pen Design

Interior design: Lori Lynch

Printed in Thailand

25 26 27 28 SET 10 9 8 7 6 5 4 3 2 1

Contents

INTRODUCTION

How to Use This Prayer Journal

Why must your first prayers for your husband have to wait until after you've tied the knot?

When I was single—tired of dating and debating whether my future husband was even out there—I turned to prayer. I'd been a believer in Jesus for many years and knew I wanted to be married for just as long. But until that point, I had merely hoped I would stumble into a happy, godly marriage. After a few heart-breaking breakups while watching other friends find their perfect match, I began to feel doubtful, dejected, and discontent. Then I realized hope on its own wasn't going to alter my mindset or affect my future marriage. I needed to plant my desire in something sure and rely on something transformative: *prayer.*

Prayer is what comforts us in all things and in every season—whether we are hopeful singles, anxious daters, or wishful women—and leads us to a posture of preparing and waiting well. Whenever I lacked vision for my future, I turned to God, and He would remind me of the promises He had written over my life and His divine design for marriage. In my time preparing, I made my own

"Husband's Bible"—a space where I could capture my prayers for my future husband and write letters for him to later read. Whenever I was tempted to settle or compromise, I would open my Bible and use it as a tangible reminder that awaiting God's plan was better than fastening on control or comfort. I wrote notes in the margins, dedicating it to my future husband. On my wedding day, I watched my husband, Arden, take every written letter and dated prayer into his hands and realized God had me in *His* hands all along. He has *you* in His hands too.

This prayer journal is for you—whether you are awaiting or approaching your wedding day—so you can be praying for your future husband. You might not know who he is yet or when he's going to come into your life. But you can start praying for him now in all the areas that matter to him as a single man. Doing so will mean so much to your marriage in the future.

Then, on your wedding day, this journal will be a gift for him—a beautiful way he can see how you cared for and prayed for him in the weeks, months, or even years before you walked down the aisle. The written record of your heart's desires and prayerful devotion will bless him again and again throughout your marriage. You'll have space within each section to write out prayers, notes, and letters to reflect on your journey as a future wife.

This is a preparatory practice. The prayers don't stop at the wedding day. In fact, I hope you'll find that by committing to prayer in this season, you're creating a holy habit of prayer that will naturally flow into your marriage, covering yourself and your husband. By enlacing your desire and dream of marriage with prayer, may you find God's pen marks all over your love story here and now and throughout your happily ever after.

I pray this journal becomes your tangible tool, a reminder of hope, and a resource to equip your thoughts and prompt your prayers for your future husband and coming marriage.

Christian Bevere

My Prayers for You

You formed my inward parts; you knitted me together in my mother's womb. I praise you, for I am fearfully and wonderfully made.

Psalm 139:13–14 ESV

1 | Pray for His *Identity*

Two individuals becoming one—what a miraculous and marvelous act!

But do we understand what that actually means? We long to be loved, to know another soul so fully that it makes us feel like we're walking on the clouds and beaming like the sun. But how can we deeply know another person, or allow them to know us, if we do not properly know ourselves? Scripture uses the Hebrew word *yada* to show how God knows us, signifying a deep relationship and an intimate understanding that moves past the surface level of familiarity toward the heart. We come to fully know who we are only through the One whose likeness we were created after.

Psalm 139 says that even before we drew our first breath, God knew us completely. He fashioned His sons and daughters, creating us in His image to bear His likeness and be examples of His love on earth. He knows what makes us laugh and cry and what causes us to feel passionate, anxious, excited, and embarrassed. He knows us thoroughly! Sometimes we're tempted to hide parts of who we are from Christ, or we have areas of our hearts reserved for other things.

But if we are found in the One who fully knows us, imagine how much more fully we will live and be able to share our hearts with our spouse!

God invites us into an identity that is larger than any one person—an identity of holy purpose and majestic magnitude. We are His handiwork, His beloved, and His illustrations to those around us. What an identity to bear! As your husband's future wife, you have the gift of praying for him to walk in that identity. Ask for divine, specific, God-given traits in your future husband's identity and that he may discover them in Christ alone.

Prayer Prompts

- Ask God for your future husband to see the unique facets He has fearfully and wonderfully fashioned within him.
- Pray for your future husband's ability to rest in God's love for him over any striving to prove himself.
- Pray that he will cast off false labels, insecurities, fears, or ill expectations that keep him from abiding in his God-given identity.
- Ask the Lord to fortify his identity so he is ready to build a strong and stable God-centered marriage.
- Advocate for God to grow him fully in the areas of his identity, making him a man of honor, honesty, and humility.
- Call on God to lead him in understanding that his identity is a chosen coheir and beloved son.

My Prayer for You:

I prayed over you on these dates:

Heart-to-Heart Homework

What Is in a Name?

In *Romeo and Juliet,* Shakespeare wrote that a rose by any other name would smell just as sweet, but there is significance in the names we use and words we speak as part of our identities. Take a moment to write the names, attributes, and blessings you'll proclaim over your future husband.

As you pray for him, declare names such as "leader" or "overcomer" or names of endearment like "my darling" or "*mi amor.*" Even though you may not know his real name yet, you can start speaking blessing over his identity!

Becoming a Future Wife

Things to Ponder

Have you let your identity be shaped by your relational status or the status you hope for?

What are your core values and unique attributes, and how do they show up in your daily life?

What legacy are you creating through the way you live?

Why do you want to get married? What is your deeper motivation?

Which qualities and features do you wish to foster most in yourself?

Make every effort to supplement your faith with virtue, and virtue with knowledge, and knowledge with self-control, and self-control with steadfastness, and steadfastness with godliness, and godliness with brotherly affection, and brotherly affection with love.

2 Peter 1:5–7 ESV

2 | Pray for His *Character*

Our character is the expression of what resides in our hearts and what we believe in our spirits. If our characters are rooted in Christ, the outworkings are fruit (or evidence) of His residency. Galatians 5:22–23 identifies this fruit as love, joy, peace, patience, kindness, goodness, faithfulness, gentleness, and self-control (ESV).

How does someone amplify fruitful character? First John 3:7 tells us that whoever practices righteousness from Christ's example *is* righteous. As we spend time with God in prayer and fellowship, we become like Him. Just as spending time in the sun brings darkened skin or listening to a song often familiarizes the lyrics, drawing near to God is how we build character.

If character is instilled, it may also be amplified through prayer. The fruit of the Spirit can grow over time in your husband, allowing you to recognize those qualities in him and providing sustenance for your marriage.

However, it's not only the husband who should exemplify godly character. Proverbs 31:10 queries, "A wife of noble character who can find? She is worth far more than rubies." As you pray for your future husband's character, ask the Lord to search your heart as well. For a heart refined and tuned to righteousness is a precious gift to your husband and a notable offering to the Lord.

Ask God to work righteousness within you as individuals and as a couple. Call on God to build both your characters, refining and growing you to be steadfast followers of the gospel and spouses for each other.

Prayer Prompts

- Ask God to shape your future husband's heart to reflect His—full of compassion, righteousness, and steadfastness.
- Request for your future husband to sense and see fruit that God is developing as he draws near to the Lord.
- Pray that the Lord will search his being and show him any area where he may be lacking and how to grow in faith.
- Pray that your future husband would understand the weight of his words and actions, asking God to open his eyes as he adopts Christ's example.
- Appeal against any type of comfort in unhealthy patterns, asking God to interrupt any area where he is not fully living out his true character.
- Call upon the Holy Spirit to make His voice heard to you and your future husband through conviction and clarity.

My Prayer for You:

I prayed over you on these dates:

Heart-to-Heart Homework

Blessing in the Fruit!

As you pray for your future husband, ask God to cultivate the fruit of the Spirit (Galatians 5:22–23) in his life. Let the accompanying scriptures guide and enrich your prayers.

Patience

Proverbs 14:29
Colossians 3:12
Ecclesiastes 7:8

Kindness

Ephesians 4:32
Zechariah 7:9
Proverbs 11:7

Faithfulness

Psalm 31:23
Proverbs 3:3-4
1 Corinthians 4:2

Joy

Romans 12:12
Philippians 4:4
Isaiah 55:12

Self-control

2 Timothy 1:7
Proverbs 16:32
Titus 2:11-12

You will know your future husband by his fruit (Matthew 7:16 and Galatians 5:22-23).

Becoming a Future Wife

Things to Ponder

How are you embodying godly character as a single woman?

What values do you hold that guide your decisions on a daily basis?

Who are you when no one else is around?

Are you generous with your time, words, and actions?

How do you treat all people, even those who have nothing to offer you?

Without faith it is impossible to please him, for whoever would draw near to God must believe that he exists and that he rewards those who seek him.

Hebrews 11:6 ESV

3 | Pray for His *Faith*

Faith is both a promise and a practice.

It is our assurance of what we hope for yet cannot see, and it is a muscle we must continually exercise to keep strong. Without it, we are wanderers, unsure of what to trust and which way to turn. Anytime we are confused or doubtful in our faith journey, we can look to Christ to find our way.

Hebrews 12:2 conveys that Jesus is the pioneer and perfecter of faith. Through His example, He's given us the unwavering hope that we can rely on God's promises and the reassurance that we can walk in faith as we wait upon them.

Faith clings to the proof you have in Him and supplies sustenance in the areas where proof cannot be found. When you say yes to Christ, you are enacting faith that He will guide you and never leave you. When you say yes to your spouse, you are relying on the good proof he has shown that he will care for and commit to you, and you are supplying faith through love that your relationship will last where there is no proof.

Faith is like a trust fall, where you must rely and release all at once.

Scripture is filled with people who required faith to hear God's voice and successfully fulfill His plans. Abraham needed faith in God's goodness when He called him to sacrifice his long-awaited son, Isaac (Genesis 22). Joshua needed faith in God's power when He called him to lead the Israelites to conquer Jericho (Joshua 6). Faith is a practice that leads to peace, a guide that directs our steps, and the requirement for allowing God to lead us toward His promises.

Pray for your future husband's faith so that he, too, will walk boldly in the ways and promises God has set before him.

Prayer Prompts

- Ask the Lord to show your future husband areas where his faith can increase and become richer.
- What lessons of authentic faith can you glean from Mark 9:14–29? Pray that posture for your future husband.
- Ask for God to make Himself known to your future husband and create a greater dependency upon Him.
- Ask the Holy Spirit to guide him as he spends time in the Word, revealing His mysteries and making His truth come alive.
- Contend for good spiritual soil for your future husband so his faith may grow complete (Matthew 13:18–23).
- Pray that the Lord would reveal any areas where he is relying on faith in himself and can begin relying on Him.

My Prayer for You:

I prayed over you on these dates:

Heart-to-Heart Homework

To the One I Have Faith Will Come into My Life

Fill in any area(s) where you are growing in faith or have experienced a surplus of faith recently. Maybe you've joined a small group and it's sharpened your faith, or you're activating faith as you walk with a friend who doesn't know the Lord yet. This exercise is intended to make you aware of the working of faith in your own life now, and later give your future husband a glimpse into your heart.

Faith is the assurance of things hoped for, the conviction of things not seen.

Hebrews 11:1 ESV

Becoming a Future Wife

Things to Ponder

How are you intentionally drawing near to God's holy presence as a consistent practice?

How is God growing your own faith through this time in prayer?

Let the Lord illuminate anywhere you may be putting your faith other than in Him.

Read and reflect on the following verses: Proverbs 3:5–6; Isaiah 26:3–4; Mark 11:22–24; and Matthew 21:22. What benefits and blessings does God's Word promise for those who live by faith?

Think of those around you who do not know the Lord. Who may God be prompting you to share your faith with?

You are a chosen race, a royal priesthood, a holy nation, a people for his own possession, that you may proclaim the excellencies of him who called you out of darkness into his marvelous light.

1 Peter 2:9 ESV

4 | Pray for His *Purpose*

Many of us wonder, *What was I put on this earth to do?*

We tend to confine our callings within our careers, but that's only one part of our purpose. Purpose cannot be boxed inside an occupation or ambition; it's a vibrant, fluid mission. Your calling is more than your occupation, last name, or religious denomination. Christ instructed His followers and disciples to walk in their calling as sons and daughters of the Most High, glorifying and working for God in *all* they did. We don't clock in and out of purpose, nor do we have to limit it to a certain square footage. It is part of everything we do, fueled by our faith in God and activated through our love for others.

Your future husband's calling is not placed within one occupation, location, or title, but placed in the one true God! Ask God to reveal His plan to him and guide him in the way He leads. Pray for a purpose that isn't swayed and doesn't run out, but one that is constantly looking for people to love and being replenished by the love God lavishes upon us.

You have been designed with a specific, unique, and God-breathed purpose. When you know your purpose in God, you can properly build upon it alongside another. So, will you rise to your true calling?

Pray that as singles, you and your future husband will stand in the purpose the Lord has for you both and be ready to walk in joint purpose when He brings you together.

Prayer Prompts

- Pray for God to reveal glimpses of your future husband's purpose to him and you, individually and collectively.
- Thank the Lord for what He has already placed in your future husband's hands. Pray that He will show him how to be faithful with what he has been called to.
- Intercede for him to develop a boldness to share the gospel and make Christ's name known.
- Pray that God will remind your future husband that his purpose and identity are in Him alone rather than what he owns or what he does publicly or professionally.
- Ask God to break your future husband's heart for what breaks His and to give him a spirit attuned to the things of the Lord that remain his anchor throughout his life.
- Request that God illuminate opportunities for each of you to walk in purpose every day.

My Prayer for You:

I prayed over you on these dates:

Heart-to-Heart Homework

Purposeful Date Nights!

Here are future date ideas and their bonding purpose. Star the ones you're most looking forward to.

Date Idea	Purpose
Write a couple's bucket list.	Capture your goals and vision for places you want to explore together, and begin saving and planning for those trips.
Try tandem rock climbing (indoor or outdoor).	Face your fears and rely on each other on this thrilling date.
Put all screens away and focus on connection.	Be fully present, just the two of you. Find new conversations to have, and overcome your reliance on screen entertainment.
Prepare a new recipe together.	Discover new flavors and build culinary skills by trying a homemade recipe for pizza or pasta.
Take a pottery or painting class.	Expand creativity and get outside your comfort zone through this fun outing.
Volunteer together.	Bond by helping others in a meaningful way, side by side.
Re-create your first date.	Rediscover what brought you together and recount what was memorable from where it all began.
Make each other a playlist that reminds you of your partner.	Pick songs that remind you of them or capture your feelings, then explain why you chose each song.
Visit a bookstore and pick a book for each other.	Connect through the arts! Introduce each other to a new favorite or explore a new genre. Enjoy being in each other's company as you set aside time to read.

Becoming a Future Wife

Things to Ponder

What ways may God be prompting you to step out in your purpose?

Ask God what He has created you to do in this season and for His help to silence the noise of any distraction in the way.

What does/will it mean to be a couple whose relationship is for and focused on the kingdom?

There are so many ways we can spend our time. Ask God to give you greater clarity on how to schedule your time over the next week.

Are there any goals or ideas that God is asking you to either lay down or pick up? Pray Proverbs 19:21 for God to sharpen your vision.

How much better to get wisdom than gold, to get insight rather than silver!

Proverbs 16:16

5 | Pray for His *Wisdom*

Wisdom is different from intelligence. While geniuses are born with an above-average IQ, and knowledge comes from tenacious seeking and studying, wisdom is a gift from God. He invites us to request wisdom whenever we need it and is ready to impart it to those who draw near and ask: "If any of you lacks wisdom, let him ask God, who gives generously to all without reproach, and it will be given him" (James 1:5 ESV).

This gift isn't for building our résumé, but rather for building a godly life! As James 3:13 declares, "Who is wise and understanding among you? By his good conduct let him show his works in the meekness of wisdom" (ESV). Worldly wisdom is shown in books, boasts, and businesses, but heavenly wisdom is shown through the way one lives.

Believers who fear the Lord, seek His guidance, and walk in humility will receive divine insight and applicable understanding. Through the gift of wisdom, your future husband's life will progress and persevere. His wisdom will bring discernment, pave the way for innovation, and guide him in understanding God's will. He will apply heavenly wisdom in the way he makes decisions, how he works, and in his processing.

Heavenly wisdom acts as a compass for our path and an anchor for our reasoning.

As you ask God for an increase of wisdom for your future husband and yourself, thank Him for all the ways it will shape your lives—even as a tool in bringing you together and bettering your marriage.

Prayer Prompts

- Bless your future husband in wisdom in all the places he may need it currently: career decisions, school, friendship choices, and so on.
- Pray that God will guard him through the wisdom He gives, leading him to make informed decisions that guide him down a good path (Ecclesiastes 7:12).
- Ask God to make your future husband a man of wisdom, showing him how to shift from acting out of habit to meditating on godly wisdom before he speaks or acts.
- Call on God to surround him with wise voices and examples.
- Request that God will give him discernment and a desire for truth.
- Pray that, despite your future husband's natural intelligence, God will make him dependent on Him for true wisdom and lead him to fear the Lord's holy presence (Proverbs 9:10).

My Prayer for You:

I prayed over you on these dates:

Heart-to-Heart Homework

Wise at Heart!

It takes a wise mind to remember little details. Here's a fun challenge to share some thoughtful insights and memories with your future spouse.

My First Memories (Fill these out during singleness or while dating.)

My first crush:

My first movie in a theater:

My first real job:

My first proud accomplishment:

My first time praying for my future husband:

Do You Remember? (Fill these out during engagement or marriage.)

What he wore on your first date:

When you realized you were in love with him:

Whether you were nervous about your first kiss:

Your first impression of him:

How he made you feel at your first meeting:

Becoming a Future Wife

Things to Ponder

James 1:5 invites us to ask for wisdom in any area where we lack it. Where would you ask God to give you a greater understanding?

Preemptively pray that God will give you wisdom in dating decisions and choices for your marriage.

The fear of the Lord is the beginning of wisdom (Proverbs 9:10). Are there any areas blocking that awe and wisdom?

How can you exercise leaning not on your own understanding (Proverbs 3:5–6)?

Seek the Holy Spirit's wise promptings throughout your day and ask Him to give you wisdom on how to pray for your future husband.

Commit to the LORD whatever you do, and he will establish your plans.

Proverbs 16:3

6 | Pray for His *Career*

Careers that honor God can come in various occupations but only one expression. Perhaps your future husband will be a stockbroker, a restaurant chef, or a deliveryman; the title he wears is less important than the *way* he wears it. We glorify the Lord in our careers when we are hardworking, honorable, and helpful.

Begin blessing him for the character to carry his calling!

Colossians 3:23 says that whatever we do we are to do it with diligence as if doing it for the Lord rather than men. Examples of men marked by their skill and dedication in the Bible include David as a shepherd, Ezra as a scribe, and Daniel in government advisement. Their lives show us that God can make a difference anywhere and through anyone! So, while you may not know which career(s) your husband will engage in, you can pray for him to be equipped for them—both in spirit and in skill.

Those who carry their careers honorably will flourish, find favor, and carry influence. As a farmer who plants in the winter brings forth fruit in the spring, following how God calls us to plant produces diligent fruit (Leviticus 26:3–5). Whatever work and endeavors you and your future husband set out to accomplish, pray for flourishing that makes way for generosity, favor that wins others over, and influence to make a difference for good.

Ask God for all your future husband will need for his career—direction, insight, favor, determination, mastery, and ability—as he is beginning his career journey or working to establish it.

The Lord is his ultimate boss, promoter, and advocate, able to place and position him where He leads. Intercede for your future husband's work and abilities, and pray that the Lord will establish him in his career.

Prayer Prompts

- Call on the Lord to grant your future husband integrity and humility in all he does, treating others as greater than himself and striving to serve as he succeeds.
- Pray for him to have favor among men and leaders (Luke 2:52).
- Ask that the Lord would shut the wrong doors while opening the right ones.
- Implore God to keep him from confusing his calling with his career, remaining in the Lord as he navigates the workforce.
- Earnestly pray for him to see purpose over status or dollar signs and for God to keep him from being prideful and from stumbling.
- Ask that God will shape his mind to see career success and wealth as a path for generosity and for supporting your future family.

My Prayer for You:

I prayed over you on these dates:

Heart-to-Heart Homework

I Believe You're Going Places

Everyone needs a little encouragement. Use this page to write a love letter to your future husband, encouraging him in his career. Tell him how you'll stand beside him through the small beginnings and big blessings. Write out the traits you've been praying over him—intelligence, favor, and boldness—that will be noticeable throughout his career.

SPECIAL DELIVERY

TO MY FUTURE HUSBAND

XOXO

Becoming a Future Wife

Things to Ponder

Remember that great avenues form from small beginnings (Zechariah 4:10). Seek endurance in your career to carry you to lasting success.

Ask the Lord to show you *His* way to success and to help you not seek shortcuts or status but lasting success.

Dedicate your passions, projects, and plans to God, and ask that He will set them into motion in the right ways and at the right time (Proverbs 16:3).

We like to work and plan—but focus on the now! Ask the Holy Spirit to direct you in what to work toward presently to avoid rush or confusion.

How can you create a greater vision for your career that will generate legacy and impact others through what you do?

We are God's handiwork, created in Christ Jesus to do good works, which God prepared in advance for us to do.

Ephesians 2:10

7 | Pray for His *Talents*

The Lord appointed you and your future husband before you ever breathed your first breath, setting you apart for amazing attributes! Jeremiah 1:7–8 reminds us not to retreat from these gifts but to press into them. Even if you both are young, inexperienced, or in an overpopulated career field, none of those things determines how effective your talents can be. That's because your talents and gifts do not rest on your own ability to increase or master them—they are God-given!

What's even greater than God giving individuals specific gifts is how these gifts come together to unite and grow us in harmony. As the body of Christ, we can use our talents to come alongside one another, complementing each other and working together for a greater purpose (1 Corinthians 12:27).

Speak blessing over your future husband for heavenly talents and giftings. These could be gifts of personality, creativity, prophecy, worship, leadership, discernment, or ability. Every gift is from the Lord and has the potential to increase and enable him to reach others. Your future husband may have exceptional craftsmanship, have an incredible singing voice, or be an amazing athlete. Whatever his talents and giftings, you get the role of asking for increase and for him to be set apart.

Proverbs 18:16 says, "A man's gift makes room for him and brings him before the great" (ESV). As a wife, someday you will watch your husband operate in his gifts up close. For now, as a wife-to-be, you can bless his abilities from afar. Contend for him to experience supernatural increase in insight, ask for him to have the heart to use his gifts for others rather than his own gain, and pray that he won't neglect or fear utilizing them.

Prayer Prompts

- Pray for your future husband to have boldness to develop and share his talents and gifts.
- Request that God will supply him with resources, teachers, and time to practice and refine his God-given abilities.
- Seek dreams, vision, and direction regarding your talents and his, and search out how to glorify God with your giftings.
- Pray that he will not experience insecurity, comparison, or small thinking when it comes to his talents.
- Appeal to God for increase for your and your future husband's talents and for instruction on how you both can benefit and bless others.
- Ask God to reveal any hidden or unused talents within that can be strengths for heavenly purposes.

My Prayer for You:

I prayed over you on these dates:

Heart-to-Heart Homework

My Hidden Talents

You've been praying for *his* talents—now it's time to reveal a few of your own!

Can you lick your elbow, do an impeccable impersonation, or hold a record for most sneezes in a row? Give your future husband a glimpse at just how talented of a wife he has!

1. ______________________________

2. ______________________________

3. ______________________________

4. ______________________________

5. ______________________________

What a *gift* it is to pray these verses over your future husband:

- *James 1:17*
- *Romans 12:6–8*
- *Matthew 25:23*
- *1 Timothy 4:14*
- *1 Peter 4:10*

Becoming a Future Wife

Things to Ponder

Pray that the Lord will grant you wisdom in how to encourage your future husband in his gifts and abilities.

What talents has God given you that you can use to inspire, uplift, or connect with others?

How will you create space for your future husband to explore his talents? Preemptively prepare for a mindset of collaboration rather than comparison in your marriage.

Even God-given abilities can be strengthened. Seek out someone who you can study under, apprentice, or be inspired by to help sharpen your craft.

How will you set a guard against competition in your talents so your and your husband's gifts complement and co-inspire each other?

Do not fear, for I am with you; do not be dismayed, for I am your God. I will strengthen you and help you; I will uphold you with my righteous right hand.

Isaiah 41:10

8 | Pray for His *Protection*

The world can be scary at times. Natural disasters, disease outbreaks, and spiritual attacks are all real perils we can face—maybe all in one day. But though we face darkness, we do not have to fear, for the Lord goes before and behind us.

God's power is our most reliable protection! During a storm at sea, Jesus slept in perfect peace, then calmed the storm with one rebuke (Matthew 8:23–27). That's the God we serve—mightier than anything you or your future husband may face.

As men, our husbands will lead the charge of protection over our homes and lives. But to be able to protect, they must know they are protected. Ask God to give him strength in trials, reliance on Him, and belief in His power and presence. Exercising authority means standing strong during the trial *and* partnering with righteousness in the calm.

Instead of focusing on what could come against you, focus on how you can come against it! Maybe you're a single woman living alone or have walked through a trying time. How have you relied on God's power and protection, and how can you use that as a testimony of faith-building by blessing your future husband?

Ask for wisdom so your future husband may walk in God's instruction rather than in harm's way; plead for discernment and boldness, and ask that he may carry the fear of the Lord over a spirit of fear. Envision your husband as a soldier. You get to help equip him with mighty prayers so he can stand tall in the wake of battle.

There is power in the name of Jesus, so call upon Him! The Lord is our refuge and fortress (Jeremiah 16:19). Make your secret place with God a shelter for protection, both now and in the days ahead.

Prayer Prompts

- Ask God to develop your future husband's faith over fear and create a stronger reliance on His name and power.
- Fortify his mind and guard his spirit by interceding on his behalf (Isaiah 54:17).
- Call on the Lord to expose spiritual threats and give him discernment.
- Pray that the Lord will grant him the understanding that we wrestle not with flesh and blood so he can effectively wage war in the right manner (Ephesians 6:12).
- Cover your future husband in the battle gear of Ephesians 6:10–17.
- Ask God to remind him that the safest place he can be is in His presence. Pray that instead of worrying, he will seek refuge within God's dwelling.

My Prayer for You:

I prayed over you on these dates:

Heart-to-Heart Homework

Holding Out for a Hero!

You likely won't come to your husband's rescue in a cape with a memorable catch-phrase, but if you were his hero protector, in what style would you "save the day"?

My superhero power would be:

Stylistically, my trademark item would be:

Is my identity hidden or public?

In real life, I'm a handy sidekick because of my ability to:

Every hero has a secret weakness; mine is:

My getaway vehicle would be:

When your superhero-like skills seem unreliable, cling to these verses to declare protection over yourself, your future husband, or a trying situation.

- *Psalm 27:3*
- *Isaiah 54:17*
- *Hebrews 13:6*
- *Exodus 14:14*
- *Philippians 4:13*
- *Romans 8:31*
- *Psalm 91:4*

Becoming a Future Wife

Things to Ponder

How can you practice relying on God and exercising authority in your current season?

Submit your time to intercessory prayer, allowing God to wake you and guide you whenever you need to pray on your husband's behalf.

Ask the Holy Spirit for a discerning spirit so you can contend in the battles you each may face now and later.

Meditate on Psalm 91:1–16. Begin praying for a calm that follows you both through any storm.

James 4:7 tells us to resist the devil and he will flee. How are you actively making the Lord's protection a first defense rather than a last resort?

You keep him in perfect peace
whose mind is stayed on you,
because he trusts in you.

Isaiah 26:3 ESV

9 | Pray for His *Peace*

We rely on peace more than we think. Peace is more than a happy feeling; it's a countenance of assurance—like a compass signaling when something is on track or off course. When something feels off, it causes us to pump the brakes and reevaluate. Like in our relationships, we don't move forward unless we feel peace when we are with the person. When a circumstance is surrounded by serenity, we sense we can continue in confidence. How do we gain a peace that is enduring and reliable? True peace, lasting peace, comes from prayer.

Whenever our peace comes from God, it is not easily stolen. Walking in His ways grants us a noticeable peace that is evident to those around us. The world can provide comforts, but only God grants lasting peace. Consider what may be robbing you of peace that you can trade for more of God's presence.

Bless your future husband with an otherworldly type of peace—a peace that makes no sense. Because that's what Christ has offered us: "Peace I leave with you; my peace I give to you. Not as the world gives do I give to you. Let not your hearts be troubled, neither let them be afraid" (John 14:27 ESV).

Peace is also an action. Laying down our whims and comforts to serve others grants us an abundance of peace. We see this when we look at Jesus, the Prince of Peace, and how He lived. He brought the promised peace to the Israelites; where they expected a radical warrior redeemer to conjure a peace that was hard-fought, He brought peace through sacrificial love that cannot be stolen.

As you prepare to live, partner, and grow together, ask God to impart in you peaceable spirits.

Prayer Prompts

- Pray for God to grant your future husband a peace that surpasses his own natural understanding (Philippians 4:7).
- Appeal to the Lord to teach your future husband how to rest in Him *before* he experiences anxiety, fear, or stress.
- Ask God to show him the way to renew his mind through His Word and what it looks like to be refreshed in His presence.
- Pray that God will remove anything robbing or blocking his peace in this season, and expose any choices or agreements he has made that may be bringing unwarranted anxiety or fear.
- Appeal to the Lord to bestow on him perfect peace as he follows His laws and keeps His commandments (Isaiah 26:3).
- Advocate that God's peace in his life would be evident to himself and others, from the way he sleeps and speaks to how he talks and thinks.

My Prayer for You:

I prayed over you on these dates:

Heart-to-Heart Homework

Time for a Trip!

There are some places where we are most at rest and peace fills us. Describe the most peaceful place you've ever been. Print a photo you took there and tape it here, or if you don't have one, draw how you remember it.

Peace is always beautiful.

Walt Whitman

Becoming a Future Wife

Things to Ponder

Matthew 5:9 calls us to be Peace-makers. Meditate on the difference of being a peace-keeper vs. maker.

Are there any areas where you can make way for peace (forgiving someone, reconciling with a friend, or healing from past hurts)?

How do you carry God's peace now? Does your countenance draw others to see God's love?

Ask the Lord to grant you and your future husband peace during your times apart so you can make the right decisions in wisdom instead of angst.

Describe a recent situation where you had to fight for peace and saw the blessing from it.

The LORD sees not as man sees: man looks on the outward appearance, but the LORD looks on the heart.

1 Samuel 16:7 ESV

10 | Pray for His *Heart*

Our hearts are incredibly determinative as believers. Yes, even mighty, stoic, rugged men rely on heavenly hearts. The heart is like our navigation system, a guide in everything we do. Proverbs 27:19 says, "As in water face reflects face, so the heart of man reflects the man" (ESV).

What we hold in our hearts, good or bad, instructs how we act toward those around us. To walk in divine love, we must guard our hearts and watch over their habitats (Proverbs 4:23). Until our hearts have been marked by God's love, they can be faulty and unreliable, leading us to act out or lash out. The state of your heart is vital in your faith, self-reflection, and relationships—current and future.

When we ask the Lord to come into our lives, we receive new hearts—ones set on the Lord—allowing us to express His commandments through compassion, forgiveness, generosity, and gratitude (Colossians 3:12). With purified hearts, we can walk with God and rely on His love to fuel our own.

As you pray over your future marriage, keep your hearts in mind. If your love has been given to things other than the Lord, ask Him to renew it and create a clean heart within you. As your love for each other brings you together, keeping your hearts rooted in the Word's instruction will *keep* you together.

Prayer Prompts

- Request that God will create a pure heart within your future husband.
- Pray that compassion will spring forth from his heart like a river and that the Lord will instruct him in kindness, sincerity, and thankfulness.
- Pray for the Lord to steward your future husband's ambitions so that they are rooted in purposeful ways, and to set his heart in a faithful direction.
- Appeal to God to keep his heart anchored in Him and not be caught in things that will lead to harm or frailty.
- Pray that as he acts purely out of love for the benefit of others, his heart will be refreshed in the Lord (Isaiah 58:10–11).
- Ask that his heart remain malleable to the Lord's instruction.

My Prayer for You:

I prayed over you on these dates:

Heart-to-Heart Homework

Here's My Heart!

Complete the phrases below to show your love-to-be some things that you adore. Whether it's a morning *sunrise* or hot *bubble baths,* share a little bit of the simple things and sweet nothings that make your heart glow.

Things that make my heart full:

Morning

Fresh

Dreamy

Slow

Hearing

Intentional

Hot

Seeing

Time

Finding

Feeling

Soft

Creating

Nights

Becoming a Future Wife

Things to Ponder

How does God's unconditional, agape love inspire you to love deeper?

Take time to meditate on all the ways God's love has transformed you.

Appeal to the Lord to guard your heart from the things or places that could hinder or hurt it (Proverbs 4:23).

For a pure and lovely heart, take the challenge to pray Psalm 139:23–24 for the next seven days.

Matthew 6:21 shares how our hearts lead our minds and will. Is anything taking too much of your heart?

How can a young man keep his way pure? By guarding it according to your word.

Psalm 119:9 ESV

11 | Pray for His *Purity*

Purity is expressed outwardly through the body but originates inwardly via our hearts, minds, and spirits. Purity presents itself as we are renewed and refreshed inwardly.

Some desires may feel all-encompassing, but we have the ability to draw on Christ to see them through. We do not need to ignore or shame our desire for love and intimate connection in order to walk in purity. Through prayer, higher thoughts, and focus, we can keep that desire within God's perfect plan.

Rather than denying our hope for romance, we fare better by entrusting it to its proper time and treatment. Imagine you're carrying something precious and breathtaking to its rightful spot. You don't want to set it down early in a place where it could be mishandled, nor should you set it aside as if it's unimportant. See it through to its proper place, where it can be admired and developed.

The biblical book Song of Solomon is a beautiful display of admiration and affection written from the viewpoint of a man and woman in love. Like a back-and-forth diary, we get a glimpse of the couple's prayers and exclamations of longing and excitement. This story shows that purity does not have to be lifeless or lacking in passion; it simply needs to be treated with honor. They did not scorn their desires but blessed and kept them within God's instruction for their marriage. You can seek purity and still get excited for what is to come. Purity is important outside of marriage but just as significant within.

How can you enlarge your view of purity from something you have to struggle to gain to something that is strengthening you and your marriage? Begin praying for your future husband's purity to guard and carry him in singleness and prepare him for a committed love and vibrant passion within your marriage.

Prayer Prompts

- Pray for a heavenly guard around your future husband's mind, heart, body, speech, and spirit so he embodies purity fully.
- Ask for God to grant you both sufficient strength to overcome temptations: *Lord, let us not be hasty or awaken love before its time* (Song of Solomon 2:7).
- Pray for conviction to work its blessing in him. Ask the Lord to speak to him when he's drifting or whenever he has misstepped.
- Pray for the Holy Spirit to speak to him when he is in wrong situations or places, leading him to run from temptation.
- Ask God to supernaturally guard him from the Enemy's schemes, such as pornography, suggestive social media, and crude talk.
- Intercede for purity in *all* his ways: his work, his relationships, his free time, and his thoughts.

My Prayer for You:

I prayed over you on these dates:

Heart-to-Heart Homework

Purity Promises

Pure love is committing to care for each other and follow God's instruction for guidance. Each season holds challenges to protecting your purity, as well as different areas and ways to do so. Complete the dialogue below by sharing how you'll chase a pure, prolonged love in each circumstance and in each season.

In singleness, I'll love you by:

In dating, I'll love you by:

In marriage, I'll love you by:

With my eyes, I'll love you by:

With my words, I'll love you by:

With my actions, I'll love you by:

With my thoughts, I'll love you by:

Becoming a Future Wife

Things to Ponder

Pray that the Lord will make your desire for a spouse pure and your actions throughout dating honorable. Ask Him to keep you from acting out of angst or lust.

The Lord gives us a steadfast spirit through purified hearts. Ask Him to wash over yours and shape it through His fashioning.

Request a vision for your marriage that is honorable to your husband, others, and God.

Ask God to show you how to keep Him as your first desire so that all other desires may follow in righteousness.

What in your own life can you remove that is leading to ill-fit love or impure thoughts (for example, types of entertainment, romance novels)?

Have I not commanded you? Be strong and courageous. Do not be afraid; do not be discouraged, for the Lord your God will be with you wherever you go.

Joshua 1:9

12 | Pray for His *Courage*

How do the brave stand unafraid or the mighty unfazed? They have *cultivated courage*. One does not become brave overnight but grows in faith to become courageous.

Before Joshua set foot into the promised land, God told him to be strong and courageous—three times, in fact. He made a point to prepare Joshua with a holy fear, so he would revere the path of the Lord, and built him up with trust. Joshua's battle preparation was largely spiritual, behavioral, and mental. After he heeded God's instructions and kept His ways, Joshua saw the city of Jericho and all Israel's other adversaries fall by the supernatural power of God.

An obedient heart and fervent spirit are the mightiest tools in our arsenal.

To find courage we must find something worth fighting for in faith and remember that the God of the universe is on our side—or rather, we get to be on *His* side! Those who are courageous stand in their authority and know where their help comes from (Psalm 121:2).

Courage can simply be a fancy word for trust.

Trusting in God's supreme plans and power will serve you and your future husband both in the midst of hardships and the stillness of waiting. So, while you're waiting to meet your husband or whenever you are together and navigating hard choices, take courage knowing that your hope, your answers, and your peace are found in the Lord who goes before and behind you.

Begin praying for your future husband's courage and that his trust in the Lord will guide and carry him.

Prayer Prompts

- Ask that God's Word and instruction would be bigger than any fear or uncertainty in your future husband's life.
- Request that the Lord sharpen him as a leader—among friends, in your family, or in his workplace—and make him an example of spiritual courage.
- Intercede for divine courage so he may stand when it's unpopular, speak when it's easier to be silent, and be courageous when it's more comfortable to shy away.
- Pray that God allows His guidance to be the reassurance your future husband needs to step into the unknown.
- Ask God to give him glimpses of the areas He has called him to conquer so he can faithfully prepare, just as David did (1 Samuel 17:40).
- Ask for God to grant him boldness in the small, everyday decisions so that he may stand firm in the larger, harder decisions to come.

My Prayer for You:

I prayed over you on these dates:

Heart-to-Heart Homework

Channeling Courage

You were brave enough to venture into the dating world and have courageously been praying over your future husband, but let's shed some light on the times your courage was still developing.

A time I overcame something scary (*for example, public speaking or surviving a natural disaster*):

My biggest irrational fears (*for example, a fear of spiders or germs*):

Thrills or challenges where my courage shines (*for example, riding roller coasters or navigating a Black Friday sale crowd*):

Becoming a Future Wife

Things to Ponder

Ask God to show you and your future husband areas where fear or doubt may be looming so that you may courageously apply faith.

Have you held fear or doubt for the future? Assess what is important to you and how it is greater than worry.

God's Spirit gives us power, love, and a sound mind. Put these promises to remembrance and action with a current decision or problem you're navigating.

Read 1 Samuel 25. How does Abigail's example inspire you to apply courage in times of distress or uncertainty?

It takes courage to believe whenever doubt creeps in. Take a minute to meditate on a time when your faith in God was met with His faithfulness.

Two are better than one, because they have a good return for their labor: If either of them falls down, one can help the other up.

Ecclesiastes 4:9–10

13 | Pray for His *Community*

A community is a group that embodies togetherness and shares commonalities. The people you surround yourself with will influence how you live, shape your beliefs, and either add or drain your energy. It's important we choose our circles with care, and I'd suggest through prayer. You can pray for the type of friends (in both of your lives) who will encourage you, stand by you on the hard days, and bring transformation.

A vital component to being a godly spouse is being in godly community. Godly community is more than friendship or companionship. These are people who are on aligned mission, carry one another's burdens, and listen and forgive one another. They're the people who can laugh with you for hours or cry it out all night. The ones who have your back and whom you can be yourself around. In true community we *become* our best and *contend* for the best.

Our communities are built through friends, family, leaders, and mentors and can develop from work, hobbies, church, or childhood. We *all* need people who are going to shoot straight with us, encourage us when we are low, and point us toward God's Word.

But finding transformation in community first requires something of us. Abraham was called a friend of God because he walked in faith and righteousness (James 2:23). When we carry these transformative attributes ourselves, we are able to carry godly friendships and even friendship with God! First John 1:7 says, "If we walk in the light, as he is in the light, we have fellowship with one another" (ESV).

Pray for your future husband to walk in righteousness so he may walk with godly friends. Ask the Lord to grow you both to become people of transformation so that you may be a blessing to your community and to each other.

Prayer Prompts

- Pray that God would give your future husband a variety of relationships—with those his age, older, and younger—that are purposeful in sharing testimony, wisdom, and joy.
- Ask for God to bring him godly community so he and his friends may encourage one another and sharpen each other to be men of valor.
- Pray that you would both be planted in a church.
- Pray for your future husband's community to share transparency so that they foster a safe space to be honest, confess sins, and process life together.
- Advocate for the Lord to show him how to serve his community through generosity, church, or outreach.
- Intercede for his eyes to be open if he is involved with any wrong community and that he would not allow untrustworthy voices into his mind.

My Prayer for You:

I prayed over you on these dates:

Heart-to-Heart Homework

You've Got a Friend in Me!

As you pray for your future husband, pray for his community as well. Contend for Godly friends in his life—perhaps they're one of these types:

The Comedian: ______________________________

He is hilarious. This is the one who always makes him laugh and may help calm any nerves on your first "meet the friends" hangout. He brings joy to your husband's life.

The Sage: ______________________________

He's a mentor or a wise older friend. He gives godly advice and is always a listening ear. This guy is well-versed and well-read, and your husband can rely on him.

The Ride-or-Die: ______________________________

He could be a childhood best friend or the roommate since college. This guy has your husband's back through and through and has serious best-man potential.

The Workout Buddy: ______________________________

He's always up to blow off some steam or play sports on a Saturday, and will probably come over for every game day. This guy is a consistent pal and an easygoing hangout buddy for your husband.

The Motivator: ______________________________

He doesn't let your husband stay in his comfort zone. Maybe he was the one who first invited him to church or pushed him to apply for his dream job. This guy sees almost as much gold in your husband as you do!

The Wild Card: ______________________________

He is always up to something new. One day he's running a marathon and the next he's going backpacking in Europe. This friend inspires your husband and adds spontaneity to his life—a little unpredictable in nature but loyal in friendship.

Becoming a Future Wife

Things to Ponder

Seek unity in your friendships and that time with friends would be profitable for uplifting and growing.

Pray for your relationships to be an example of iron sharpening iron—not allowing room for gossip, comparison, or idleness.

Take a deeper step to foster godly community: Seek a mentor, join or start a small group, or find someone with whom you can share your testimony.

Is there an area you have been missing out on community (ex: canceling plans, skipping celebrations, or missing church)? Make, and keep, plans in that area this week.

How is your community enriching you, and how are you growing together?

Be completely humble and gentle; be patient, bearing with one another in love. Make every effort to keep the unity of the Spirit through the bond of peace.

Ephesians 4:2–3

14 | Pray for His *Family*

The day you're connected with your future husband, you connect families as well. His loved ones get to become your loved ones, and later you may get to create your own little loved ones. As a couple, your family enlarges to become a harmony of both of you as your own family unit, your immediate families, and your growing family. This is no small act! Nor is it without purpose.

The Bible weaves an understanding that we are not our best by ourselves. It's through relationship that we ward off isolation and its blind spots. In unity we become stronger, experience God's presence, and find power in prayer.

Family denotes more than a bloodline, it signifies a powerful connection of mind, body, and beliefs. Even the body of believers is referred to as a family.

To be joined together—through blood or by marriage—is a gift.

Through family we grow in our faith and increase in our joy. When we embrace and enjoy the blessing of family, we bring a world of gladness to ourselves and also can show the world the essence of God's love. Jesus Himself prayed, "They may be brought to complete unity. Then the world will know that you sent me" (John 17:23).

Begin praying for your future husband's family—for a strong bond and unity that reflects how God desires us to connect.

Prayer Prompts

- Pray that the Lord will teach your future husband what it means to be a faithful son, father, husband, brother, and uniter.
- Request that God show you both how to honor your parents and love your sibling(s).
- Ask for God to give him a father's heart before you have children.
- Pray that the Lord will establish legacy within your marriage and family, whether building anew or upon existing foundations.
- Contend for salvation for any unsaved family members.
- Wherever there has been strife or conflict in family dynamics, ask God to soften your hearts and bring you both patience to mend the rift and create unity.

My Prayer for You:

I prayed over you on these dates:

Heart-to-Heart Homework

Say Cheese!

As you bond, bringing two families together and establishing your own new family unit, celebrate the joy and capture the smiles. At your wedding, over holidays, or on vacation, take photos and commemorate these new beginnings and relationships. Print your favorite photo and paste it here!

Becoming a Future Wife

Things to Ponder

Begin blessing your future in-laws now and believing in a seamless and genuine relationship among you.

What lessons in love and connection have you learned from your own family? Are there any areas in which you need mending or a new direction?

Begin praying for your future husband and children. Ask God to give your heart patient expectation and joyous gratitude for them.

Interview a couple who's modeled marriage and family well and ask them what they've learned and enjoyed most throughout their marriage.

You and your husband will come from two different backgrounds and upbringings. How will you contend for understanding as you blend two worlds together?

Praise the LORD, my soul, and forget not all his benefits—who forgives all your sins and heals all your diseases, who redeems your life from the pit and crowns you with love and compassion.

Psalm 103:2–4

15 | Pray for His *Health*

Health can be viewed as a depleting asset, but with God it's not so! In Him, health can be rejuvenated and redeemed.

Has fear of asking the wrong way or doubt of the unknown kept you from believing in healing? The same Lord who wove you together in your mother's womb can restore you to health. He is the all-powerful God—nothing is too great for Him! He may bring healing through an instantaneous miracle or at the hands of physicians, or He may give you wisdom for lifestyle or dietary changes, but one thing is for sure: He is able.

Some pain points may not be completely healed until we are in eternity. While there are accounts like the woman with the issue of blood receiving instant healing, there are others like Jacob who carried a limp his entire life—but both of these people operated in faith. Health is greater than an ache-less body; true health is when faith flows through our veins, thoughts, and hearts—enabling us to rely on God in our weaknesses.

The healthiest state we can be in is devotion.

In our crying out for and receiving of health, let us walk by faith! Begin speaking God's Word and believing His goodness. God is our healer, Jehovah Rapha, and is able to heal what we bring to Him and even other areas He may bring to us. Ask God for health in your bodies, minds, and spirits and for Him to show you any area He wants to rehabilitate.

For your future husband, for yourself, for your marriage—invite God's supernatural power into your circumstances and anoint your present and future with His rejuvenation.

Prayer Prompts

- Ask God for longevity and stability in your future husband's health so he may be fit and able for the call on his life.
- Plead the blessings and promises of Psalm 103 over him now, covering him head to toe.
- Cast off fear of health hazards and hidden threats and ask God for wisdom in how to live in health (Psalm 91).
- Pray in the name of Jesus that any current or future addictions, insufficiencies, and diseases that would seek to harm your future husband are canceled.
- Plead that God would lead each of you in a mindset of obedience and discipline over comfort so you may eat and live in ways that honor your bodies as temples of the Holy Spirit.
- Contend for full health—mind, body, and spirit—for your future husband so he may live in fullness.

My Prayer for You:

I prayed over you on these dates:

Heart-to-Heart Homework

Help Build Healthy Habits

We can bring one of two options into our marriage: health-building or health-hurting habits. Let's choose the former! Here are a few to set you up well:

Physical

Get adequate rest.

Spend time outside daily.

Eat whole foods and limit sugar intake.

Mental

Practice taking deep breaths when stressed.

Journal for processing and reflecting.

Make your bed each morning.

Spiritual

Spend time in the Word four or more days a week for transformation.

Fast from digital devices.

Practice frequent, positive self-talk.

Social

Laugh with friends often and talk beyond surface-level topics.

Balance your yeses and noes.

Practice gratitude and celebrate small wins.

Additional healthy habits I'm being intentional with are:

Becoming a Future Wife

Things to Ponder

Even in our discomfort and suffering, Christ is with us. Pray that God would show you purpose, connection, and peace even in times of ailment or weakness.

John 10:10 says Jesus came to give us full life. Are there any areas in your body or mindset that are not operating in fullness?

What miracles have you witnessed or experienced that fueled your faith?

How has God touched your own health—mental, physical, or emotional?

Reflect: What do you need to overcome in order to believe that God does and can heal?

Instead, whoever wants to become great among you must be your servant, and whoever wants to be first must be your slave—just as the Son of Man did not come to be served, but to serve, and to give his life as a ransom for many.

Matthew 20:26–28

16 | Pray for His *Leadership*

Jesus showed a new way of leadership through servanthood, flipping authority on its head. He showed that He seeks leaders of spirit and heart over fervor or wit alone, desiring to uplift men and women who show people the kingdom way versus those who seek to get their own.

King Saul, Judas Iscariot, and King Ahab were all influential in their own ways but found their downfall when they put themselves first. In contrast, men such as Joseph, Nehemiah, and the prophet Samuel showed power and influence by serving God and others. What you lead with affects the leadership you carry. Lasting, peaceful, transformative greatness comes from being someone who honors the Word and honors others.

Your future husband can be a great leader!

Ephesians 5:23 says that the husband is the head (*kephalē*) of the wife. This Greek word also communicates the meanings: "source," "authority," and "leader." To be a leader, especially in a marriage, is to take on a great responsibility. Your husband will walk in front of you to guard and protect you; he will lead the charge in practical matters and spiritual battles; and he will carry a concealed weight for accountability for you both. A husband's authority does not determine that his wife is powerless or subordinate; rather, it identifies a way that men rely on their wives to aid them in their roles as visionaries and leaders.

As future wives, we can preemptively aid our future husbands' leadership through prayer.

Start blessing your future spouse now by asking God to give him a servant's heart, vast humility, and knowledge of His truth. These will shape the way he leads his life, those under his leadership in work or society, and your home.

Prayer Prompts

- Pray that God would teach your future husband profound integrity and humility.
- Ask the Lord to make him a resilient forerunner, and remind him when he feels low that he is more than a conqueror in God (Romans 8:37).
- Call upon God to mark your future husband's leadership with divine characteristics—boldness, wisdom, trustworthiness, and faithfulness—so that he can give Him the glory.
- Advocate for God to keep him from stumbling blocks such as pride, the desire for instantaneous gain, anger, and bitterness.
- Pray that God would give him a heart for those he is called to lead—showing instruction and correction through guidance over dominance.
- Pray that reverence for the Lord will remain your future husband's compass for how he leads those around him.

My Prayer for You:

I prayed over you on these dates:

Heart-to-Heart Homework

Part of Being a Leader Is Being Vulnerable

It's time for you to be vulnerable and express to your future husband how you see and honor him as a leader through one of these three methods:

1. Draw a picture.
2. Write a poem.
3. Create a collage.

Through the method you select, show an example of his role as a leader. Maybe you'll draw him in his role or career, write beautiful lines about how you believe he is a leader, or make a collage of words or verses that you believe will mark his leadership. The goal is to creatively and playfully compliment and encourage him.

Becoming a Future Wife

Things to Ponder

Study female leaders from the Bible, such as Deborah, Priscilla, and Lydia. What qualities in them inspire the way you lead?

To lead well, godly husbands need wives who also possess leadership qualities. What attributes of a leader have you been equipped with?

Pray for God to give you boldness to lead in the spaces He has placed you, like Esther and Miriam, even when you feel unqualified or unseen.

Ask God to give you a vision for the kind of environment and marriage He's calling you to help build.

As a leader, how do you serve and help steer those in your life?

Do not conform to the pattern of this world, but be transformed by the renewing of your mind. Then you will be able to test and approve what God's will is—his good, pleasing and perfect will.

Romans 12:2

17 | Pray for His *Mind*

There are so many places our minds can wander: *What is the point in trying for that job I don't stand a chance of getting?* or *Why did I embarrass myself like that?* or *Oh no, did I turn off the oven?* Since negative or distracting thinking can so readily fill our brains, it's pertinent we fill our minds with powerful and profitable thinking!

Through prayer and reflection, we remain alert—focusing our attention and hope on the *right* things. What exactly should our minds be set to? Philippians 4:8 says, "Whatever is true, whatever is noble, whatever is right, whatever is pure, whatever is lovely, whatever is admirable—if anything is excellent or praiseworthy—think about such things."

Keeping to the best things means we guard our minds against what is not best.

Help make your future husband's mind a fortress! Pray that any thoughts that could distract, tempt, or taint him will be blocked. Intercede on his behalf, asking for him to have a refreshed mind of renewal and insight.

By tuning out the noise of the world, we can better tune in to the mind of Christ. Being led by His Spirit and counsel, our minds become instruments set to usher in His heavenly instruction and echo His goodness. When we are His, our minds are on Him. God says, "I will put my laws in their minds and write them on their hearts. I will be their God, and they will be my people" (Hebrews 8:10).

Pray for your future husband's mind to be set on Jesus and remember His ways.

Prayer Prompts

- Ask for God to fill your future husband's mind with gold: problem-solving, creative thinking, and intelligence.
- Request that his mind be guarded from negative self-talk and unprofitable thoughts.
- Pray to the Lord that whenever your future husband's thinking is troublesome or misguided, he will be encouraged to renew his mind in Christ.
- Ask God to grant him mental clarity and focus, guarding him from distraction or doubt.
- Pray that God will give him His peace, which transcends all understanding, instead of him feeling the weight of the world and stress from a racing mind (Philippians 4:7).
- Ask God to supply him with all the mental attributes he needs to lead a profitable life: a clear mind, resolve, and rational, analytical thought.

My Prayer for You:

I prayed over you on these dates:

Heart-to-Heart Homework

Show Him How Your Mind Works!

Answer the questions below to share a glimpse into your way of thinking:

1. Something I think is funny is:

   ____

2. A conspiracy theory I believe is:

   ____

3. I think ______________________________ is overrated, and ______________________________ is underrated.

4. ______________________________ is the best book of all time.

5. I believe I could give a TED Talk on:

   ____

6. The most valuable lesson I learned from my childhood was:

   ____

7. The best way to spend a weekend is:

   ____

8. My most redeeming quality is:

   ____

9. I think the first thing I'll notice about you will be:

   ____

10. I believe the best part of our marriage will be:

    ____

Becoming a Future Wife

Things to Ponder

As you pray for your future, keep your thoughts anchored in the present so you do not drift too far ahead and miss what God is speaking to you and showing you now.

Where do you tend to feel stuck or confused? Have you invited God into your thought process?

Assess your mental forefront. Are you taking thoughts captive often and effectively (2 Corinthians 10:5)?

What unfruitful mental habits can you release today (for example, overthinking, anxiety, doubt, and comparison)?

What scriptures and truths have been transformative for your mind?

We also glory in our sufferings, because we know that suffering produces perseverance; perseverance, character; and character, hope. And hope does not put us to shame, because God's love has been poured out into our hearts through the Holy Spirit, who has been given to us.

Romans 5:3–5

18 | Pray for His *Perseverance*

Enduring through seasons of waiting, trials, or temptations creates a steadfastness that other seasons cannot produce.

Whenever we choose to keep going, though it may be easier to throw in the towel, we grow in spiritual maturity and in our relationship with Christ. Scripture encourages us to endure hardships because doing so leads to character, which leads to hope, which leads to stronger faith (Romans 5:1–5). This is because perseverance reminds us that God's grace sustains us through all circumstances: "Blessed is the one who perseveres under trial because, having stood the test, that person will receive the crown of life that the Lord has promised to those who love him" (James 1:12).

The instantaneous nature of the modern age can cause us to rely on momentary motivation versus persevering in pursuits. But as believers, we are called to push on rather than stop or slow down. Maybe your single or dating seasons have required patience and steadiness, but that can work toward your benefit. Biblical wisdom shows that fruitfulness is ahead when we stay the course and do not despise the paths that begin with small beginnings or longer timelines. The apostle Paul said in his letter to the Galatians, "Let us not become weary in doing good, for at the proper time we will reap a harvest if we do not give up" (6:9).

When trials feel heavy, goals are slow to be achieved, or seasons come that test your future husband's strength and patience, hard-won perseverance will help him rise to the occasion and remain victorious. Let your prayers support him to *keep going*—in faith, hope, and endurance.

Prayer Prompts

- Pray for your future husband to persevere whenever he feels weak by tapping into God's supernatural strength and endurance.
- Ask the Lord to give him foresight that overcomes any anxiety and patience that fuels his passions.
- Ask God to teach your future husband resilience by guiding him through times when he faces testing, disappointments, or challenges.
- Contend for the Holy Spirit to guide him to work *with* his weaknesses instead of striving *only* in his strength and giving up when he feels unable (Romans 8:26).
- Appeal to the Lord to give your future husband dreams, words, or direction for the right paths so he doesn't use his willpower and energy to chase the wrong goals and desires.
- Pray for him to have friends and community that stick with him in the hard seasons and encourage him to keep going in the right direction.

My Prayer for You:

I prayed over you on these dates:

Heart-to-Heart Homework

Better Each Day!

Practice makes *perseverance.* Let's find all the ways you can push through with determination in this season. Choose a box (or two or three!) and cross it out once you have completed the task.

- [ ] Learn a new skill or hobby you've always wanted to try.
- [ ] Make plans for a coffee meetup, then keep your commitment *and* show up on time.
- [ ] Keep a plant alive for a month.
- [ ] Spend five days without makeup and find an attribute you're grateful for each day.
- [ ] Build a piece of furniture without giving up.
- [ ] Go an entire week without acting upon road rage.
- [ ] Choose a new workout regimen and follow it for the next two or three weeks consistently.
- [ ] Save 30 percent of your income for a month.
- [ ] Make coffee at home for an entire week.
- [ ] Practice pronouncing a difficult word like *Worcestershire* or *onomatopoeia* and use it in three conversations.
- [ ] Wake up before six a.m. for a week . . . without snoozing the alarm!
- [ ] Challenge yourself to buy healthy groceries and eat dinner at home seven nights in a row.
- [ ] Complete a fast.
- [ ] Have a conversation with family members or friends and be mindful to listen instead of speak.
- [ ] Finish a 500- or 1,000-piece puzzle.

Reflect

What did some of these habits teach you about yourself?

Did they establish new habits or routines you're now putting into practice?

Becoming a Future Wife

Things to Ponder

Ask God to grow your strength in quiet places, teaching you to endure even when it's hard and to rely on His power over your own.

Develop a habit that teaches you discipline and delayed reward (for example, a fitness regimen, learning a new skill, or saving money).

How can you seek joy in the delays and build endurance to keep praying for what you're hoping for?

What actions can you take now to encourage perseverance and discourage angst (for example, fasting from social media or journaling your dreams)?

Was there a time you needed supernatural endurance? How did it build your faith and determination?

Therefore, if anyone is in Christ, he is a new creation. The old has passed away; behold, the new has come.

2 Corinthians 5:17 ESV

19 | Pray for His *Past*

Your past is no match for your future!

Especially in our relationships, we can believe our futures to be crippled by our pasts. But by God's mercy that is not so! If we confess and repent of our sins, those past mistakes lose their power over us as we trade that space for God's power. In the book of Isaiah, God said, "Forget the former things; do not dwell on the past. See, I am doing a new thing! Now it springs up; do you not perceive it? I am making a way in the wilderness and streams in the wasteland" (43:18–19).

Everyone—yourself and your future husband included—has fallen short in some way. There may be things from your past you'd like to blot out from your story. But rather than pretend the past didn't happen, we can learn from it and find release from its grip on us. Shame says we are bound to what we did or what others did to us, but the truth proclaims that we are liberated by what Christ did for us! "This I call to mind and therefore I have hope: Because of the LORD's great love we are not consumed, for his compassions never fail. They are new every morning; great is your faithfulness" (Lamentations 3:21–23).

Do you believe the promise that you and your future husband are both new in Christ and that you can create future legacies as He leads you (2 Corinthians 5:17)? Pray with belief that it is so and walk in that freedom!

Prayer Prompts

- It's time to throw out the old and make way for the new! Ask for the fruit of the Spirit to replace the areas sin once occupied in your and your future husband's lives.
- Pray that the Lord will help you each acknowledge your mistakes and overcome them so you may walk in complete freedom.
- Pray for any past temptations or sins to have no power over him now and for his mind to be fortified by the promises and protection of the Word.
- Plead for God to teach him how to release shame and separate who he is from what he has done, giving him faith to believe that God is the ultimate repurposer (Isaiah 61:7).
- Pray for God to lead him to people he can confess to and heal alongside, those who are accountability partners and wisdom-givers.
- Ask God to allow you each to be inspired by His forgiveness, allowing you to love each other richly because you understand how much His love transformed your own lives.

My Prayer for You:

I prayed over you on these dates:

Heart-to-Heart Homework

Practice Putting the Past Behind You

In Jesus we have freedom and a future. The apostle Paul said, "You once were dead in your trespasses, but now you're alive in Christ" (Ephesians 2:1, 4–5, paraphrase)! We can live unashamed by who we were because we know without a doubt we are made new in Him. Here you will identify what once was and declare what is and is to come.

In the first box, write out any areas you once struggled in and then cross them out. In the second box, write out who you now are and are continually becoming in faith. (For example, "I was addicted and lost" becomes "I am found and forgiven.")

I was

I am

If the Son sets you free, you will be free indeed.

John 8:36 ESV

Becoming a Future Wife

Things to Ponder

Meditate on 2 Corinthians 5:17. As a new creation in Christ, how does your present differ from your past? What new behaviors and habits do you hold?

Could there be any ways you're limiting your future because you believe you are unworthy or undeserving due to your past?

Ask the Lord to guide you to fully forgive yourself for past mistakes and receive His grace to walk in a new path according to His merciful redemption.

With a close friend, recount how God rescued you from a time of trouble, sin, or hopelessness in the past. Note how you recall and experience God's redemptive power.

Think of the ways you speak to and see yourself; then contemplate Hebrews 8:12 and Isaiah 43:25. Are you still holding yourself in bondage or have you released the past?

I know the plans I have for you, declares the Lord, plans for welfare and not for evil, to give you a future and a hope.

Jeremiah 29:11 ESV

20 | Pray for His *Future*

Everything you're doing now has a purpose. With prayer as our navigation system, our steps become clearer and more focused on God's purpose. You may have a five-year plan or larger-than-life goals, but have you asked the Lord what He has in store for you? The wisdom found in the book of Proverbs says this: "Many are the plans in a person's heart, but it is the LORD's purpose that prevails" (19:21).

There is a path of purpose ahead for you and your future husband. And you can be sure that you do not have to find it on your own or fulfill it in your own strength! Even what may feel like two steps back while following God is forward progress in His instruction. Because it is not by your own know-how or ability that you step into a future of significance and success, but by continuous guidance and direction from the Holy Spirit. He is good to give us a hopeful future and faithful to see us to it. The apostle Paul observed that "he who began a good work in you will carry it on to completion until the day of Christ Jesus" (Philippians 1:6).

What lies ahead of you is laced with impact. The surest way to days of peace, actions of influence, and a life of legacy is by laying down what we think we should do or hope to do and lifting His name above our own.

Pray for your future husband to prevail, prosper, and thrive where the Lord leads him. Ask that every step be faith-building or lesson-learning. As you rely on God for your path, your husband's path, and a path that unites you, celebrate that God wove a future unique and special for you specifically as His beloved daughter.

Prayer Prompts

- Pray that God would give your future husband a mind set on trusting Him for all he is believing for in the coming days and years.
- Ask the Lord to bless the work of his hands, the vision in his mind, and the well-being of his soul so he may walk forward earnestly and expectantly.
- Petition God to begin planting seeds of future dreams, glimmers of hope, and continual growth that will bring a plentiful harvest in his future.
- Pray that the Lord will give him patience for what lies ahead, not rushing anything but heeding its revealed time.
- Ask God to set him apart for signs and wonders, things that have never been done before.
- Pray that God will make you both like gold utensils for His glory—set apart and fit for use!

My Prayer for You:

I prayed over you on these dates:

Heart-to-Heart Homework

Dreaming of Our Future

Begin to write out dreams for your future. These can be fun experiences and adventures you hope to have, trips you want to take, ideas you can explore as a couple, challenges you can conquer together, or longings from your heart in regards to family or the impact you hope to have in the world.

Cast a vision for your future together. One day you'll look back on your dreams and see how many have come to pass and which to keep pressing toward.

ADVENTURES

CHALLENGES

VISIONS

Becoming a Future Wife

Things to Ponder

There's no time like the present! What are you doing today that will prepare you for the future you envision?

What dreams has God written on your heart that you can begin planning for or praying into?

Ask the Lord to give you wisdom to choose what is right over what is easy and to help you hear His voice clearly.

Pray that the Lord will help you align your path to His will rather than to the world's pressures, opinions, or ways.

Reflect: How has your trust in God's plans deepened throughout this prayer journey?

My Vows to You

This is the day you have been praying for. As you prepare to join together, reflect on your time in prayerful expectation and all God has inspired within you. Marvel at His goodness and guidance and let that inspire your vows to your beloved.

On Our Wedding Day

Date

Dear future husband,

With love,

Letters and Notes

We know and rely on
the love God has for us.
God is love. Whoever lives
in love lives in God,
and God in them.

1 John 4:16

Two are better than one, because they
have a good return for their labor: If
either of them falls down, one
can help the other up.

Ecclesiastes 4:9–10

The LORD God said, "It is not good for the man to be alone. I will make a helper suitable for him."

Genesis 2:18

Dear friends, let us love one another, for love comes from God. Everyone who loves has been born of God and knows God.

1 John 4:7

Encourage one another and build each other up, just as in fact you are doing.

1 Thessalonians 5:11

So they are no longer two, but one flesh. Therefore what God has joined together, let no one separate.

Matthew 19:6

And now these three remain: faith,
hope and love. But the greatest
of these is love.

1 Corinthians 13:13

Love is patient, love is kind. It does not envy, it does
not boast, it is not proud. It does not dishonor others,
it is not self-seeking, it is not easily angered,
it keeps no record of wrongs.

1 Corinthians 13:4–5

Let love and faithfulness never leave you; bind them
around your neck, write them on the tablet of your
heart. Then you will win favor and a good
name in the sight of God and man.

Proverbs 3:3–4

And over all these virtues put on love,
which binds them all together
in perfect unity.

Colossians 3:14

Many waters cannot quench love; rivers cannot sweep it away. If one were to give all the wealth of one's house for love, it would be utterly scorned.

Song of Solomon 8:7

Above all, love each other deeply,
because love covers over a
multitude of sins.

1 Peter 4:8

My beloved is mine and I am his;
he browses among
the lilies.

Song of Solomon 2:16

Be devoted to one another in
love. Honor one another
above yourselves.

Romans 12:10

If I have the gift of prophecy and can fathom all
mysteries and all knowledge, and if I have a
faith that can move mountains, but do
not have love, I am nothing.

1 Corinthians 13:2

That is why a man leaves his
father and mother
and is united to his wife,
and they become one flesh.

Genesis 2:24

No one has ever seen God; but
if we love one another, God
lives in us and his love is made
complete in us.

1 John 4:12

Love and faithfulness meet together; righteousness and peace kiss each other.

Song of Solomon 8:7

My command is this: Love
each other as I have
loved you.

John 15:12

Whoever pursues righteousness and love finds life, prosperity and honor.

Proverbs 21:21

About the Author

Christian Bevere is a creative communicator, author, and podcast host. Known for her relatable and transparent voice, Christian shares timeless truths through her popular podcast, *Dear Future Husband*, her YouTube channel, and her multiple books, including *Break Up with What Broke You*. She passionately engages in meaningful conversations about faith, identity, and relationships. She resides in Nashville, Tennessee, with her husband, Arden, and their two children. She continues to inspire others to live by faith and cultivate beauty.